D0593846

With blessings to my friend

Mindy

I thank God
for the gift of your friendship.

May God bless you and keep you
And make His face shine brightly upon you
Today and always.

Thanks for the gift of you!

Your Friend,

Cindy

_2008_

date

a little book of

hugs ™

for
friends

Inspiration for the Heart

**Andrews McMeel
Publishing**

Kansas City

ISBN-13: 978-0-7407-1182-4
ISBN-10: 0-7407-1182-2

Library of Congress Catalog Card Number: 00-102158

Messages by Caron Loveless
Personalized Scriptures by LeAnn Weiss
Interior design by LinDee Loveland and Vanessa Bearden
Project Editor: Philis Boultinghouse

Contents

Friends are angels who
lift our feet when our
own wings have trouble
remembering how to fly.
—Unknown

joyful
friend

*L*ook for My
splashes of *joy*.

Laughter is good medicine—
it's a great "shock absorber"
for life's unexpected bumps.

It helps take the
monotony out of
everyday life.

Don't miss out on the
continual feast of a
cheerful heart.

You'll see that a **happy** heart
bubbles over
into a **smile.**
And it's *contagious!*

Love,

Your *God of Joy*

—Proverbs 17:22; 15:13–15

F—a *friend* never *fails* to be *faithful*, even when others *falter*. She won't say, "You're *fat*" (even if you are) or *focus* on your *flaws*. She is the *first* to point out your *finest features*. A *friend* will *fortify* your *fragile frame*. She will *free* you to *flourish*. A *friend* will never *forsake* you.

R—a friend is a *rare* and *ready rock* you can *run* to in the *rain*. She will *rescue* you from *rushing rivers—regardless*. She will *revive* your heart, *refresh* your soul, and *reassure* you of *rapid recovery*.

I—a friend is not *impatient* or *impolite*. She will *inquire* about your day and *include* you in her plans. She will *identify* your most *incredible ideas* and *ingenious innovations*. A friend is *interesting*, *inspiring*, and *indispensable*. She is the keeper of your most *intimate* secrets.

E—a friend is a friend till the *end*. She is *eager* to listen and *easy* to talk with. She's your most *energetic encourager*. A friend will *embrace* you *even* in the midst of your most *embarrassing encounters*.

N—a friend will *not nag* (unless it is absolutely *necessary*). *Naturally*, she knows your deepest *needs* and is also *nice* enough to *nudge* you when you're *neglecting* your *nest*, being too *nosy*, or contemplating *nonsense*.

D—a friend is *devoted*
and *dependable*. Her *destiny*
is to *divert* you from *defeat*,
and her *devices* for *depression*
usually involve the *delicious*.
It's a friend's *divine duty* to
drown your *disappointments*
and *dispose* of your *dismay*,
and many times she *does* it
in a most *delightful* way!

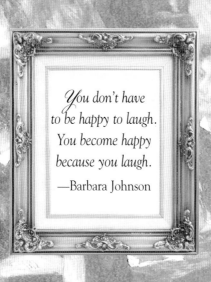

*You don't have
to be happy to laugh.
You become happy
because you laugh.*

—Barbara Johnson

two

any-weather
friend

I've chosen you!
You are *holy* and *loved*.

May you consistently live
your life with a **heart**
of compassion,

daily demonstrating *kindness*,
humility, *gentleness*,
and patience.

Choose to *gracefully*
forgive others when they
disappoint you or hurt you—

just as My Son, Jesus,
forgave you.

Most importantly, let love be
the superglue that bonds all your
relationships and friendships.

Love,
    Your *God of Love
      and
Forgiveness*

—Colossians 3:12–14

One of the best things about having a good friend is all the grace you get. You just sit around being you, and a good friend makes you think she wouldn't dream of having it any other way.

For instance, you can have a rotten attitude and end up saying things you're sorry for later, and a good friend will hardly be fazed by it.

She'll act like it's no big deal. She'll just put her arm around you and say, "Don't worry about it. Everyone has a bad day now and then"— even if you've had ten bad days in a row.

And a good friend isn't surprised by your mistakes. She expects them. Somewhere, fairly early in the relationship, a good friend will find out the truth about you. She'll witness your weaknesses firsthand. And it's at this point that your friend, if she's really a good friend, will decide to stick by you anyway.

Oh, in the early days she may have whined and complained a bit about your less-than-desirable traits, but before long, something grows in her and outweighs them—it's called *grace*.

Then, instead of fussing about your ten-thousandth tardiness, she just plans for it. She brings a book or buys a paper or files her nails. And when you finally come racing up, out of breath, with a million and one excuses, she looks at you, smiles, and says,

"Don't worry about it.
Really. It's okay. I haven't
been waiting that long."

The face of a friend reflects
God's grace.

Real friends are
those who, when
you've made a fool
of yourself, don't feel
that you've done a
permanent job.
—Erwin T. Randall

*steadfast
friend*

Catch a glimpse
of My *incredible*
love for you!

I pray that you, being rooted
and established in love,
may have the power to
grasp how **wide**

and *long*

and **high**

and **deep**

is My completely

unconditional love for you—

a *love* that surpasses all
human knowledge.

My forever love,

Jesus

—Ephesians 3:17–19

Friends possess remarkable keys. They open the locked doors of our lives. They give us entrance to places we'd never dare go by ourselves. They fling wide the gates of lush, secret gardens. They take us to treasure rooms glistening with gifts we're sure we don't deserve.

Friends unlatch the windows of our souls. They grip the drapes we've drawn around ourselves and yank them back to let God's gleaming light stream in. They pull and tug until the windows pop open and fresh, new breezes fill our musty hearts.

When storms throw trees across our path, a friend will lend her strength to haul the logs away. Friends are not fazed by our roadblocks. They come equipped with chain saws.

They help us chop our obstacles like firewood then strike a match to them. They make sparks fly up from the flames. They say, "Why not sit awhile and warm yourself by this nice fire?"

When the smoke clears, friends pass out coat hangers and feast with us on roasted marshmallows until the last ember dies.

Friends have sight where we are blind. They are guides through the jungles of our past. They are fearless to face the dangers we know lurk beneath the brush.

Friends hack and slash at the wild, clinging thoughts that bind us. With grace, they loose us from our blindfolds then tie them on branches, marking a trail for the future.

Friends create breakthroughs. The best ones are agents of God. Like Him, they stand us in front of a mirror and introduce us to ourselves.

A genuine friendship is a heavenly present. It blesses our hearts because God's love is in it.

—Evelyn McCurdy

Treat your friends as you do your pictures, and place them in their best light.

—Jenny Jerome Churchill

four

empathetic
friend

Prayer summons Me!

Where two or more of you
come together
in My name,

I am there with you.

The prayers of a
righteous person are

powerful and
effective.

Seek Me eagerly
and you *will* find Me!

Love,

Your

Heavenly

Father

—Matthew 18:20;
James 5:16; 2 Chronicles 15:15

Right away, from the very first week, God seemed to know that the world would be too wild and wooly for us to make it on our own.

He looked at Adam's single self and announced: "It's not good for man to be alone." Then He went to work and fashioned a friend for him named Eve.

When Noah came along
and the rain became a flood,
God knew Noah would be
going through some pretty
rough waters. So He sealed
Noah up in the ark and brought
his family along for the ride.

God gave Joshua to Moses as a companion for his journey through the wilderness. For forty years they walked and talked and checked their maps, until finally they found the Promised Land.

Daughter-in-law Ruth was God's gift to Naomi after the rest of her family had died.

In young David's most
desperate hour, the Lord
found Jonathan to be exactly
the kind of friend David
needed to make it to safety.

And even as His only Son traveled dusty roads and sailed stormy seas, God flanked Jesus with faithful friends and followers.

The Father knew we couldn't make it on our own either. So He birthed us into families. But He doesn't stop there. Once we've been born again, He sets us up with a loving community that laughs with us and cries with us and prays us on to forever.

To live in prayer
together is to walk
in love together.

—Margaret Moore Jacobs

five

faithful
friend

My Precious Child,

My all-seeing lamp searches
out your very *spirit* and
your **inmost** being. I
know the real you that you
sometimes try to hide.

I perceive your thoughts
and even know what
you are going to say
before you say it.

If only you realized how
precious you are to Me!

I'm continuously thinking
good thoughts of you—
thoughts that outnumber
all the grains of sand in the
entire world.

Thinking fondly of you,

Your Creator

—Proverbs 20:27; Psalm 139

A *true friend*—

...*will listen* for hours to your
   side of the story and never
   once require the facts.

...*will tell* everyone how great
   you are, even when you've
   hurt her feelings.

...*never doubts* you love her,
   even though you haven't
   called her in eight months.

...*stocks* her pantry with your
   favorite foods.

...*knows* your middle name
but will only use it when
she absolutely has to.

...*will not embarrass* you in
public.

...*will tell* you to freshen your lipstick then kindly loan you hers.

...*will always come* when your car breaks down.

...*always has* so much to tell
 you, even though you've
 known each other for thirty
 years.

...*will go* shopping for herself
 but come home with a gift
 for you.

...*carries* a good picture of you in her wallet.

...*remembers* wonderful things you did as a child, even though she wasn't there to see them.

...*would never talk* behind your
   back even though she'd
   have plenty to say.

...*will tell* you things you really
   need to hear, whether you
   feel like hearing them
   or not.

...*comes* to you with precious
messages like an
ambassador from God.

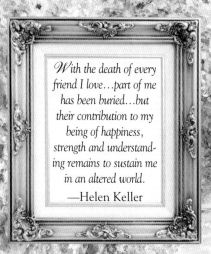

*W*ith the death of every
friend I love…part of me
has been buried…but
their contribution to my
being of happiness,
strength and understand-
ing remains to sustain me
in an altered world.

—Helen Keller

I never intended for you to
be a lone ranger.

You were *designed*
for relationship.

A friend increases your yield,
helping you reach the
potential I've destined
for you.

When you **fall**,
your friend is right there
to help you up.

Pity the person who doesn't have anyone to **stand** with her in hard times.

But a three-cord strand with Me at the center is not easily **broken**. Not even during earth-shaking, life-and-death trials.

Love,
Emmanuel,
God with You

—Ecclesiastes 4:9–10, 12

Look for these other little *Hugs* books:

A Little Book of Hugs for Sisters
A Little Book of Hugs for Mom
A Little Book of Hugs for Women
A Little Book of Hugs for Teachers
A Little Book of Hugs to Encourage and Inspire

Also look for these full-size *Hugs* books:

Hugs for Women
Hugs for Friends
Hugs for Mom
Hugs for Kids
Hugs for Teachers
Hugs for Sisters
Hugs for Those in Love
Hugs for the Hurting
Hugs for Grandparents
Hugs for Dad
Hugs for the Holidays
Hugs to Encourage and Inspire